CONTENTS

BASIC RECIPES

CAKE AND BISCUITS

BEAT AND MIX PLAIN CAKE

This recipe quantity will make one 200-mm (8-in) square cake. Refer to the *CAKE QUANTITIES* table to find approximate quantities for the round and rectangular cakes, and cup cakes, that feature in this book.

200 g (7 oz) plain flour (375 ml)
15 ml (1 tbsp) baking powder
175 g (6 oz) sugar (200 ml)
125 g (4 oz) margarine or butter
125 ml (4 fl oz) milk
3 eggs
few drops of vanilla essence

Line cake tin with greaseproof paper. Heat oven to moderate (170 °C, 325°F, gas mark 3). Sift dry ingredients together. Cream margarine or butter in a bowl and add dry ingredients, milk, eggs and vanilla essence. Beat for 3 minutes at low speed with electric mixer or for 5 minutes with egg-beater, until well blended, then pour into tin and bake for 30 to 35 minutes or until well risen and firm to touch. Cool for 5 to 10 minutes in tin before turning out onto cake cooling rack.

BIRTHDAY BISCUITS

This recipe makes 15 to 20 65-mm (2¾-in) round biscuits. Spices or alternative flavourings may be added as desired.

150 g (5 oz) plain flour
30 g (1 oz) cornflour
2.5 ml (½ tsp) baking powder
90 g (3 oz) margarine
90 g (3 oz) caster sugar
25 ml (5 tsp) milk
few drops of vanilla essence

Grease a baking sheet and heat oven to hot (200 °C, 400°F, gas mark 6). Sift flour, cornflour and baking powder together. Cream margarine and caster sugar until light and fluffy. Mix in milk, vanilla essence and flour mixture. Knead lightly. Roll out thinly (3 mm (⅛ in) thick) on floured board and cut with knife and cardboard template or with shaped cutter. Bake for about 8 minutes until golden brown. Leave biscuits on baking sheet for 5 to 10 minutes before placing on cooling rack with an egg slice.

TEMPLATES: To transfer a biscuit pattern to the dough, make a template by copying pattern onto cardboard or stiff paper and cutting it out. Place this template on rolled out dough and cut around it.

ICING

ROYAL ICING

Royal icing is used for all piping work such as piped flowers, floodwork and linework, as used in biscuit decoration.

1 egg white
200 g (7 oz) icing sugar, sifted

3 drops acetic acid or 2.5 ml (½ tsp) lemon juice
food colouring (see *COLOURINGS* below)

Place egg white in a clean glass bowl and beat until slightly frothy. Add half icing sugar, 25 ml (5 tsp) at a time, and beat thoroughly. Add acid or lemon juice. Add remaining icing sugar, 25 ml (5 tsp) at a time (you may not need all the sugar), beating thoroughly, until mixture has the consistency of well-beaten cream and forms small peaks. To colour royal icing, add a touch of paste colour on the end of a toothpick to final mixture.

COLOURINGS: Various forms of food colourings are available, including water-soluble powders, pastes and liquids. Any of these can be used successfully in butter and royal icing and in modelling pastes. Use cocoa powder to make brown butter icing, but use liquid or paste colouring to make brown royal icing and modelling paste. It is wise to test for your desired colour intensity by adding a little colouring to a teaspoon of icing or paste mixture.

BUTTER ICING

Butter icing is ideal for spreading over the surface and sides of a cake, for joining sections of cake together and for piping stars*, shells*, basket weave* and lines*. If *white* butter icing is specified for a cake, use white margarine, otherwise the icing will have a cream colour.

125 g (4 oz) margarine or butter
500 g (18 oz) sifted icing sugar
5 ml (1 tsp) flavouring
milk, water or fruit juice to mix

Cream butter thoroughly. Gradually add icing sugar. Add flavouring and beat well. Mix in a little milk, water or fruit juice until you have a smooth, spreading consistency.

MODELLING PASTES

The modelling pastes listed below can be used to create a wide variety of attractive novelties and cake decorations. Store the pastes in plastic bags in an airtight container. Do not keep them in the refrigerator as they will become hard and unworkable.

500 g (18 oz) sugarpaste
10 ml (2 tsp) gum tragacanth

Mix ingredients thoroughly.

MARSHMALLOW PASTE

NOTE: Quantities are approximate.

10 marshmallows
100 g (3½oz) sifted icing sugar
cornflour

Knead icing sugar into marshmallows, using your fingers, until a firm, elastic 'dough' is achieved. Colour as required. Roll out with a small roller or shape as desired. Use cornflour to prevent paste from sticking to hands.

DECORATING AIDS:

Lollipops
Sugared almonds
Wafer biscuits
Ginger nut or similar biscuits, 50 mm (2 in) in diameter
Ice-cream wafer cones
Marshmallows
Spaghetti
Coloured sweets
Chocolate vermicelli

*See Decorating Techniques for instructions

CAKE MIXTURE QUANTITIES		
Beat and mix plain cake:		
one recipe quantity = 20 to 24 cup cakes		
CAKE	SIZE	RECIPE QUANITY
King of jungle	200-mm (8-in) round	2 cups
Alphabet	300 x 225-mm (12 x 9-in)	3 cups
Kitten	deep 175-mm (7-in) round	1½ cups
	175-mm (7-in) round	½ cup
Sports car	300-mm (12-in) square	5 cups
	150-mm (6-in) round	1 cup
Bo-peep	175-mm (7-in) bowl	⅔ cup
Have a ball	250-mm (10-in) square	3 cups
Ballerina	2 x 200-mm (8-in) square	4 cups
Spaceship	225-mm (9-in) round	1 cup
	150-mm (6-in) bowl	⅔ cup
	3 large cup cakes + 3 spare	⅓ cup
Happy holidays	250-mm (10-in) round	2 cups
Mouse	300 x 225-mm (12 x 9-in)	3 cups

Cake making and decorating equipment:
1 square cake tin
2 cup cake tins (patty pans)
3 round cake tins
4 cake boards
5 biscuit cutter
6 large, smooth-bladed knife
7 modelling paste roller
8 paper piping bags
9 piping tubes
10 biscuit templates
11 cocktail sticks
12 paintbrushes
13 modelling tool
14 craft knife

DECORATING TECHNIQUES

— CUTTING UP THE CAKE —

1 Trace or draw cake pattern onto paper (any sort, except newspaper, can be used) and enlarge. Cut around outline, then attach pattern to cake with cocktail sticks.

2 Cut up cake, using edge of pattern as guideline and keeping knife at right angles to the board. Remove pattern.

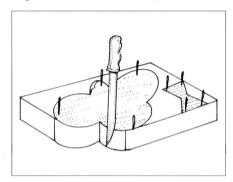

—SPREADING BUTTER ICING—

1 Soften icing with a little milk, water or fruit juice. Spread over cake.

2 To smooth, use even pressure and draw smooth-bladed knife, without lifting it, across surface. Dip knife in boiling water for easier spreading.

—————PIPING—————

Piping is best done with the aid of easy-to-make paper piping bags which can be used with any type of icing tube or nozzle. Icing syringes, which are supplied with a limited set of icing tubes, can also be used.

PAPER PIPING BAGS

Making a piping bag

1 Use squares of good quality greaseproof paper (NOT waxed paper). A 250-mm (10-in) square of paper will make two easy-to-hold piping bags.

2 Cut diagonally across square to produce two triangles. (Each triangle may be cut in half for smaller-sized piping bags.)

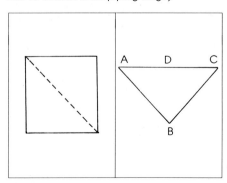

3 With long side of triangle facing away from you, roll point C to meet point B, then do the same with point A.

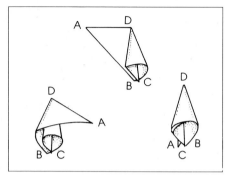

4 Fold points A, B and C inwards several times to hold layers of piping bag in place.

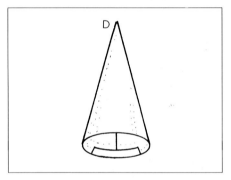

Filling the piping bag

1 Cut off point of piping bag approximately 15 mm (¾ in) from tip.

2 Drop an icing tube or nozzle into piping bag, so that half of tube extends from tip.

3 Let piping bag rest in the circle made by your thumb and forefinger and place a small amount of icing into it with a knife. Avoid getting icing on edge of piping bag.

4 Press upper edges of piping bag together and fold over the rim.

5 Fold in the corners, then seal rim firmly by folding it over several more times. A piping bag can be refilled with the same mixture two or three times.

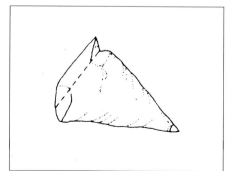

Using the piping bag

1 Once piping bag is filled with icing and sealed, hold it firmly in one hand, as you would hold a pencil. Use the whole hand and fingers to apply even pressure while piping icing onto cake (use your free hand to help guide tube).

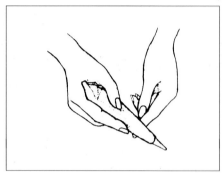

2 When you are not using your filled piping bag, place the end of the tube in a damp cloth to prevent icing from hardening and blocking tube. Do not allow the cloth to touch piping bag or the paper will soften and tear.

PIPING TUBES

A large selection of piping tubes is available from kitchenware departments in large stores or from specialist cake decorating shops. Each manufacturer uses a different numbering system for its tubes. For simplicity, one brand, Ateco, has been used throughout this book. To find tube number equivalents for the other major brands, refer to the *PIPING TUBES* table. The three basic types of tubes required for the cakes in this book are *star tubes*, *writing tubes* and *ribbon tubes*.

To make your cake decorating easier, stock up with more than one of each type of tube. You will then not need to clean the same tube each time a new colour is required.

PIPING TECHNIQUES

Lines and dots

1 Lift writing tube away from surface while applying even pressure to piping bag. Keep tube at 45° angle to surface.

NOTE: Lines and dots can also be piped using only a piping bag with the tip cut off according to thickness of line or dot required.

Leaves

1 Squeeze paper piping bag, holding leaf tube at a 45° angle; ease pressure and lift tube away.

2 Leaves are also made using a piping bag with the tip flattened and cut into a V-shaped point.

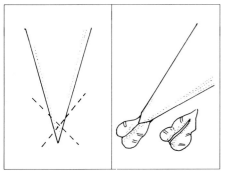

Shells

1 Using star tube, squeeze paper piping bag firmly to make icing fan out into a full base. Keep tube at 45° angle to surface.

2 Relax pressure.

3 Stop pressure and pull tube away.

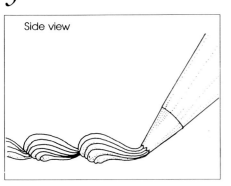

Side view

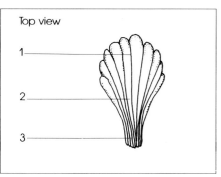

Top view

1 ————
2 ————
3 ————

Stars

1 Squeeze piping bag, holding star tube at a 90° angle; stop pressure, lift tube away.

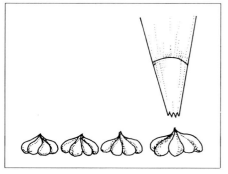

Basket weave

1 Using ribbon tube, follow steps below.

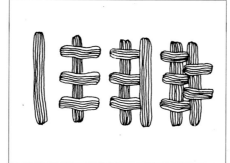

Piped flowers

1 Pipe flowers onto sheet of waxed paper using star or piped flower tube.

2 Squeeze, keeping tube at a 90° angle; stop pressure; lift tube away.

3 Add dot centre, using writing tube or paper piping bag with a very small hole.

4 When dry, remove flowers from paper.

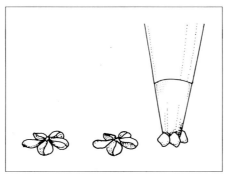

NOTE: To achieve a whirled petal effect, squeeze and twist piping bag simultaneously. Add dot centre.

MODELLING

THREE-DIMENSIONAL FIGURES AND FLAT SHAPES

Use one of the recipes for modelling pastes on page 3. Start with a ball of paste and work it between palms of hands or with fingers. Mould into three-dimensional figures. For flat shapes, roll out paste, thinly or thickly, using a small roller. (Lift paste frequently to prevent it from sticking to board.) Cut flattened paste into shapes using a template (see *BIRTHDAY BIS-CUITS*) or commercial cutters. Dry shapes on a flat or curved surface as desired.

NOTE: Small rollers can be made from a section of PVC tubing or chrome towel rail (available from your hardware store), or bought at a kitchenware or specialist cake decorating shop.

MODELLING LOLLIES

This is a simple way to make attractive novelty faces using lollipops and modelling paste.

1 Make a 15-mm (¾-in) ball of modelling paste and press it onto front of lollipop.

2 Mould paste around lollipop edges and smooth surface, rubbing gently with palm of hand.

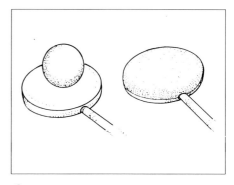

3 Shape ears or other features and accessories (e.g. hats) with your fingers, starting each object with a ball of paste. Attach features to face by dampening slightly with water and pressing into position.

4 Paint facial details using food colouring and a fine paintbrush.

FLOODWORK BISCUITS

Shaped biscuits flooded with royal icing make a colourful birthday treat.

1 Pipe outline and details of desired pattern using fairly firm royal icing* in a paper piping bag with a writing tube. Pipe separate outlines for each different colour section.

2 Working with one colour at a time, soften remaining icing with a little water and place in piping bag. Cut off tip to required size opening.

3 Flood outline, keeping tip of piping bag buried in icing all the time. (When flooding adjoining sections – either with different colours or to create distinct panels in the same colour – allow one section to set before flooding the next. This prevents icing from spilling over and merging with next section.)

See Basic recipes/Decorating Techniques for instructions

PIPING TUBES			
Tubes, and equivalents, used in this book:			
BRAND	STAR TUBES	WRITING TUBES	RIBBON TUBES
Ateco	16, 18, 33	1, 2, 4	98, 47
Bekenal	6, 7, 8, 37	1, 2, 3	22
Probus	6, 7, 8, 13	1, 2, 3	12, 9, 34
Tala	6, 7, 8, 13	1, 2, 3	12, 34

KING OF THE JUNGLE

Prepare a roaring party feast with this lion's face cake, elephant and giraffe biscuits and chewy crocodile novelties.

THE CAKE

1 x 200-mm (8-in) diameter round cake*
  40-mm (1½-in) deep
2 ginger nut biscuits (or similar biscuits,
  50 mm (2 in) in diameter)
butter icing*: 675 g (1½ lb) golden yellow;
  45 g (1½ oz) brown; 100 g (3½ oz) white
2 cup cakes*

275-mm (11-in) round cake board
6 paper piping bags
tubes: Ateco No. 4 writing, No. 18 star

1 Cut cake diagonally as shown, to form two equal halves.

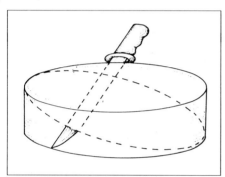

2 Turn top half of cake around so that the two thicker edges lie together.

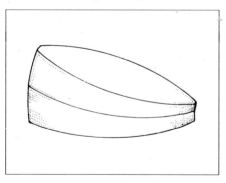

3 Soften 100 g (3½ oz) yellow icing and spread over top of cake. Smooth with a knife dipped in boiling water.

4 Position cup cakes on face to form muzzle and attach with butter icing.

5 Attach ginger nut biscuits to head to form ears, packing a little butter icing beneath them to raise them slightly.

6 Mark eyebrows and outline of eyes using a cocktail stick, then pipe in with brown icing and No. 4 tube.

7 Using white icing and No. 18 tube, pipe stars* on cup cake muzzle. Pipe dots and mouth with brown icing and No. 4 tube.

8 Place some brown icing in a piping bag and cut off tip 5 mm (¼ in) from point. Pipe large dot for nose.

9 Soften white icing to flooding consistency with water. Using piping bag with tip cut off, pipe centre of ears and whites of eyes. Soften brown icing and pipe centres of eyes.

10 Cut 10 mm (½ in) off tip of piping bag filled with softened, golden yellow icing and pipe a circle around edge of each ear. Smooth icing with knife if necessary.

11 Use golden yellow icing and No. 18 tube to pipe lion's mane (add more colouring to vary shade of mane, if desired). Start piping mane around base of cake where it rests on board: touch tube to cake, squeeze piping bag firmly so that icing adheres to cake, then pull tube away from cake to leave a tapering yellow strand.

12 Continue to pipe yellow strands around lion's head until entire side of cake is covered. Pipe final strands on surface of cake, up to dotted line marked on pattern.

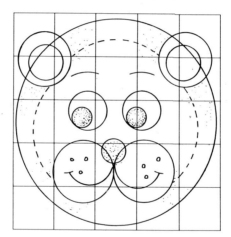

CROCODILE

250 g (9 oz) marshmallow paste*, coloured
  green
royal icing*: 30 g (1 oz) white; 30 g (1 oz)
  black
cornflour

craft knife or small, sharp scissors
2 small paper piping bags

1 Roll 20-mm (1-in) diameter ball of modelling paste into a 75-mm (3-in)-long sausage which tapers at either end. Use cornflour to prevent paste from sticking to hands.

2 Pinch top of sausage to form crocodile's back and a ridge along its tail. Pinch a ridge on the head then divide it to form eyes.

3 Roll four small sausages to make legs. Flatten one end of each sausage and cut to form toes. Dampen other end and attach legs to body.

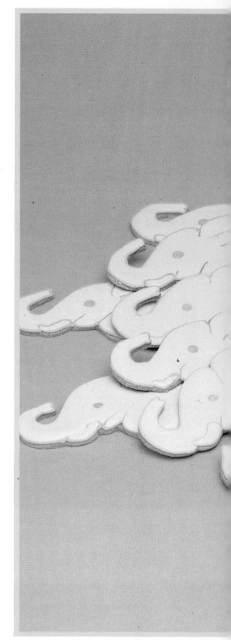

4 Use knife or scissors to slit snout horizontally, forming mouth. Make small slits on tail.

5 Open mouth wide and pipe teeth, using white icing in a piping bag with tip cut off. Close mouth to desired position.

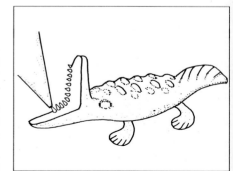

6 Pipe a black dot on top of a white dot to make eyes. Pinch end of snout and make two small hollows for nostrils. Curve tail slightly. Leave to dry.

ANIMAL BISCUITS

10 birthday biscuits*, cut and baked in animal shapes (use commercial biscuit cutters or make templates*)
royal icing*: 60 g (2 oz) brown; 175 g (6 oz) yellow; 175 g (6 oz) pale blue

3 paper piping bags
tube: Ateco No. 2 writing

1 Pipe outline on each biscuit, using appropriate colour.

2 Flood* each biscuit using thinned royal icing. Pipe on other details.

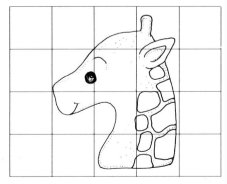

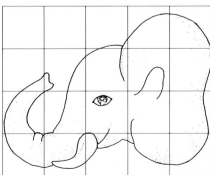

A B C D E

 F

 G

 H

 I J

 Z Y

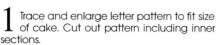

ALPHABET CAKE

From Andrew to Zoe, there is an attractive alphabet cake for every birthday child. Number cakes for every age can be made in the same manner.

THE CAKE

1 x 300 x 225-mm (12 x 9-in) rectangular cake*
butter icing*: 675 g (1½ lb) brown; 350 g (12 oz) white; 350 g (12 oz) light orange

350 x 250-mm (14 x 10-in) rectangular cake board
sharp, smooth-bladed knife
4 paper piping bags
tubes: Ateco No. 4 writing, No. 18 star

1 Trace and enlarge letter pattern to fit size of cake. Cut out pattern including inner sections.

2 Place cake on board and pin pattern to cake with cocktail sticks. Cut vertically into cake around pattern, taking care not to cut deeper than 15 mm (¾ in) below cake surface. Do not cut out inner section (centre triangle of A). Remove pattern.

3 Starting at top left-hand corner, slice horizontally into cake at a depth of 15 mm (¾ in) until you reach outline of letter. Remove this section of background. Repeat this process, cutting inwards from top right-hand corner, then from centre of base.

4 Spread softened brown icing thinly over inner sections to form background to letter. Lay pattern on cake and mark outline of inner section of letter with cocktail stick. Remove pattern.

5 Pipe outline around surface of letter with brown icing and No. 4 tube. Pipe diagonal lines, 40 mm (1½ in) apart, across surface and sides of letter.

6 Fill alternate bands between lines with white stars* piped with No. 18 tube. Fill remaining bands with orange stars piped with No. 18 tube.

7 Pipe stars over background and sides of cake with brown icing and No. 18 tube.

BLACKBOARD BISCUITS

10 birthday biscuits*, cut and baked in blackboard shape (use template*)
royal icing*: 175 g (6 oz) brown; 45 g (1½ oz) white

2 paper piping bags
tube: Ateco No. 1 writing

1 Outline and flood* biscuits. Allow to set. Pipe name of child onto biscuit using white icing.

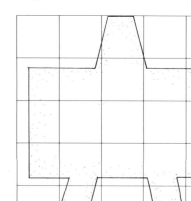

 K

 J

 L

 S R  Q  P O  N M

KITTEN IN A BASKET

This delightful cake, accompanied by flower basket cup cakes and kitten lollies, will provide a delicious birthday spread.

THE CAKE

2 x 175-mm (7-in) round cakes* – 1 x 35-mm (1¼-in) deep and 1 x 60-mm (2½-in) deep
butter icing*: 675 g (1½ lb) pink; 450 g (1 lb) white (use white margarine); 100 g (3½ oz) brown (use cocoa powder)

225-mm (9-in) round cake board
2 wooden skewers or two long pieces of spaghetti
4 paper piping bags
tubes: Ateco No. 4 writing, No. 18 star, No. 98 ribbon
6 pieces of spaghetti, each 75-mm (3-in) long

1 Place deep cake on board, and cut up shallow cake as illustrated.

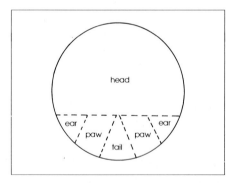

2 Attach head and paws to top of deep cake layer with butter icing.

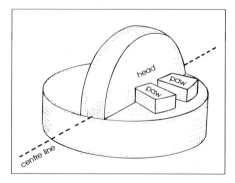

3 Attach ears to head using skewers or spaghetti for support, then soften a little pink butter icing with water and smooth onto fronts of ears.

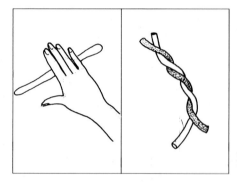

4 Cover paws, back and sides of head and ears, and top of deep cake layer with white stars* using No. 18 tube.

5 Attach tail to cake with icing and cover with white stars.

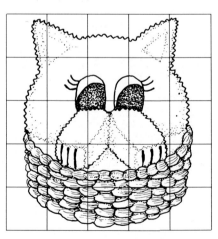

area covered with stars

6 Soften a little white icing with boiling water and smooth across front of kitten's face to form whites of eyes. Mark in eyes with a cocktail stick. Pipe outline of eyes and centre with brown icing using No. 4 tube.

7 Pipe white stars over remaining uncovered face and complete kitten by piping eyelashes and claws using brown icing and No. 4 tube.

8 Decorate sides of deep cake with pink basket weave*, using No. 98 tube. Finish rim of basket with a pink shell* border using No. 18 tube.

9 Attach piped flowers (from *CUP CAKE FLOWER BASKETS* below) to cake as desired and insert three 75-mm (3-in) lengths of spaghetti into each side of face.

CUP CAKE FLOWER BASKETS

10 cup cakes*
100 g (3½ oz) modelling paste* in white and assorted colours
butter icing*: 100 g (3½ oz) white; 45 g (1½ oz) green (leaves*)
royal icing*: 60 g (2 oz) each assorted colours (piped flowers*)

3-4 paper piping bags
tube: Ateco No. 33 star (piped flowers)

1 Make basket handles by rolling pieces of modelling paste into thin sausages about 125-mm (5-in) long.

2 Twist pairs of different-coloured sausages together. Lie handles flat and curve them to fit tops of cup cakes. Cut off excess length and leave handles to dry.

3 Attach dry handles to baskets with butter icing and decorate tops of cup cakes with leaves, piped with a V-cut piping bag, and piped flowers.

KITTEN LOLLIES

10 lollipops
200 g (7 oz) marshmallow paste*
black colouring

modelling tool
fine paintbrush (3/0 or 5/0)
1.5 metres (1½ yards) narrow, coloured ribbon

1 Follow instructions for modelling lollies* and make face, ears and nose.

2 Paint details of face with black colouring, then tie ribbon around top of lollipop stick.

YELLOW SPORTS CAR

Brighten up a birthday with this dashing car, biscuit road signs and tasty traffic lights.

THE CAKE

1 x 300-mm (12-in) square cake*, 35 to 50-mm (1¼ to 2-in) deep

1 x 150-mm (6-in) diameter round cake*, 35 to 50-mm (1¼ to 2-in) deep

butter icing*: 100 g (3½ oz) pale blue (use white margarine); 225 g (8 oz) brown; 675 g (1½ lb) yellow; 75 g (2½ oz) white

350 x 250-mm (14 x 10-in) cake board

5 paper piping bags

tubes: Ateco No. 4 writing, Nos. 16 and 18 star

1 Cut 300-mm (12-in) square cake in half, then cut one half to make two quarters. Cut one quarter (150-mm-square, 6-in square) to measure 150 x 100 mm (6 x 4 in).

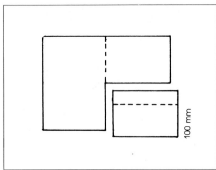

2 Cut front and back edges of half cake (300 x 150 mm, 12 x 6-in) at an angle as shown.

This forms body of car. Cut 150 x 100 mm (6 x 4-in) piece at an angle to form windscreen.

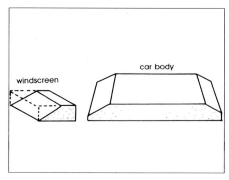

3 Attach windscreen to top of car body with butter icing.

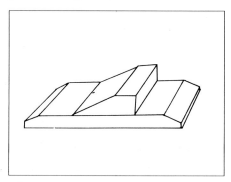

4 Cut round cake into front and back bumpers.

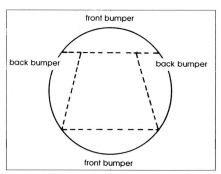

5 Attach bumpers to car with icing. Trim where necessary.

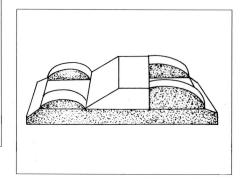

6 Cut 2 x 60-mm (2½-in) diameter circles from remaining round cake. Split each circle in two to make four wheels and attach to car with butter icing.

7 Cut two small triangles from remaining cake to make front lights and attach with icing.

8 Spread softened, pale blue icing (use boiling water) onto windscreen and back and side windows. Spread softened brown icing onto wheels.

9 Outline windows, lights, radiator and doors with brown icing and No. 4 tube.

10 Cover body of car with yellow stars* using No. 18 tube, and pipe hub on each wheel.

11 Pipe brown stars with No. 16 tube to form tyre treads, then pipe row of brown stars with No. 18 tube around base of car.

12 Pipe white stars, using No. 16 tube, to make car headlights.

TRAFFIC LIGHTS

100 g (3½ oz) white modelling paste*
butter icing*: 150 g (5 oz) brown
Smarties (or other coloured sweets): red,
   orange, green
5 wafer biscuits

1 paper piping bag
tube: Ateco No. 18 star

1 Roll ten white marshmallow paste balls, 20 mm (1 in) in diameter, into 75-mm (3-in) long sausages to form traffic light poles. Allow to dry.

2 Pipe three circles in brown butter icing, using No. 18 tube, along the top third of the front of each pole. Press one red, orange and green Smartie into each circle centre to form traffic lights.

3 Cut five wafer biscuits in half. Onto each half, pipe four circles of brown icing, one circle on top of the other, to form traffic light base. Gently push a pole into each base and allow to set.

ROAD SIGNS

10 birthday biscuits*, cut and baked in
   appropriate shapes
royal icing*: 90 g (3 oz) each red; white; blue

2-3 paper piping bags
tube: Ateco No. 2 writing

1 Pipe details and outline and flood* each biscuit using desired colours.

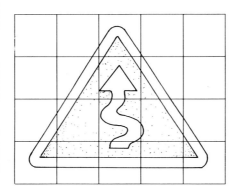

CHEVRONS

10 wafer biscuits
butter icing*: 225 g (8 oz) brown; 225 g
   (8 oz) yellow

2 paper piping bags
tube: Ateco No. 18 star

1 Pipe alternate brown and yellow stripes onto wafer biscuits, starting with yellow star at centre of lower edge.

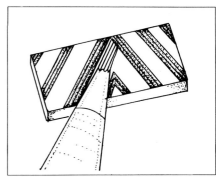

LITTLE BO-PEEP

Bring a nursery rhyme to life for the birthday child with this lovely stand-up cake and the fluffy marshmallow sheep.

THE CAKE

1 x 175-mm (7-in) diameter (at widest surface) dome-shaped cake*, baked in oven-proof bowl, 150-mm (6-in) deep
100 g (3½ oz) white sugarpaste (available from specialist cake decorating shops)
butter icing*: 350 g (12 oz) pink; 45 g (1½ oz) brown; 125 g (4 oz) white
about 15 g (½ oz) brown modelling paste*
royal icing*: 90 g (3 oz) each yellow; white; pink (piped flowers*)

250-mm (10-in) round cake board
doll, 225-mm (9-in) tall
6 paper piping bags
tubes: Ateco No. 2 writing, No. 16 and 18 star, No. 33 star (piped flowers*)

1 Place cake, top surface down, on board. Knead plastic icing until pliable.

2 Remove doll's legs and place doll on top of cake. Secure doll with plastic icing, smoothing icing up to her waist to form top of skirt.

3 Soften 45 g (1½ oz) pink butter icing with a little boiling water and spread over cake. Smooth icing with a knife dipped in boiling water.

4 With pink butter icing and No. 16 tube pipe stars* onto doll to form bodice and sleeves of dress.

5 Using brown butter icing and No. 2 tube pipe outline of apron and pockets on skirt.

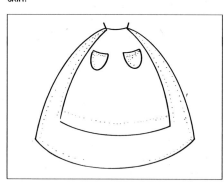

6 Pipe white butter icing stars, using No. 16 tube, around base of cake to form frill, and within outlines of apron and pockets.

7 With pink icing in No. 18 tube, pipe stars over rest of skirt.

8 With brown icing and No. 2 tube pipe dots around edges of sleeves and on apron, 10 mm (½ in) from bottom edge. Pipe buttons.

9 Make a crook by rolling a 200-mm (8-in) long sausage of brown modelling paste and curving it into crook shape. When dry, tie ribbon around top and fix crook in position on cake, using butter icing.

10 Attach piped flowers* where desired.

MARSHMALLOW SHEEP

10 white marshmallows
butter icing*: 350 g (12 oz) white; 45 g (1½ oz) black

scissors
40 x 35-mm (1¼-in) lengths of wooden skewer or lollipop stick
2 paper piping bags
tubes: Ateco No. 2 writing, No. 16 star

1 To make sheep's head, dip blades of scissors in boiling water and cut 5-mm (¼-in) slice off each marshmallow. Make two V-shaped cuts on either side of slice to form ears and chin. Keep one cut-out section for tail.

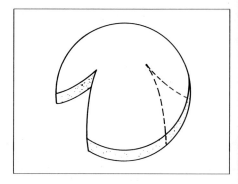

2 Push four 35-mm (1¼-in) sticks into marshmallow body to form legs. Twist sticks backwards and forwards as you push them in to ensure that they are firmly inserted.

3 Pipe stars* over entire body using white icing and No. 16 tube.

4 Attach head and tail to body with icing and pipe eyes and mouth with black icing and No. 2 tube.

"HAVE A BALL"

Treat the young football enthusiast to a goal-scoring cake and cookies with a bounce. Alternative patterns and appropriate colours can be used for other favourite sports.

THE CAKE

1 x 250-mm (10-in) square cake*
butter icing*: 450 g (1 lb) white; 75 g (2½ oz) black; 150 g (5 oz) red

300-mm (12-in) square cake board
5 paper piping bags
tubes: Ateco No. 4 writing, Nos. 16 and 18 star

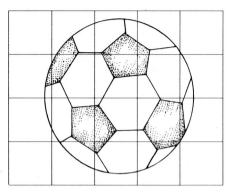

2 Attach T-shirt pattern to cake surface with cocktail sticks. Carefully cut cake around pattern, keeping knife vertical.

3 Soften 30 g (1 oz) white icing and spread thinly over area where ball will be. Leave to set for several hours.

4 Prick holes through ball pattern where lines of ball markings meet. Place pattern on iced area and transfer markings by gently pricking cake through holes in pattern (use minimum pressure or icing will stick to pattern). Remove pattern.

5 Pipe all lines on ball using black icing and No. 4 tube.

6 Use red icing and No. 18 tube to pipe sleeve cuffs and neckband, moving the tube in a zigzag motion.

7 With white icing and No. 18 tube pipe stars* over rest of T-shirt and sides of cake.

8 Pipe stars on white patches of ball using white icing and No. 16 tube.

9 With black icing and No. 16 tube pipe stars on black patches of ball.

10 Should you wish to, pipe "Have a ball on your birthday" around ball on T-shirt, using red icing and No. 4 tube.

PATTY PAN CAKE BALLS

10 cup cakes*, baked in rounded patty pans
butter icing*: 350 g (12 oz) divided into appropriate colours.

3 paper piping bags
tubes: Ateco No. 2 writing, No. 16 star

1 Turn cup cakes over so rounded surface is uppermost.

2 Football: With brown or black icing and No. 2 tube pipe lines of ball according to pattern. Pipe stars* on white and black patches of ball using No. 16 tube.

3 Rugger and other balls: Spread softened icing in appropriate colour over cup cake. Pipe lines or laces with No. 2 tube.

1 Trace T-shirt pattern and enlarge it to measure 250 mm (10 in) at widest point. Trace football pattern and enlarge to measure 90 mm (3½ in) in diameter. Cut out patterns.

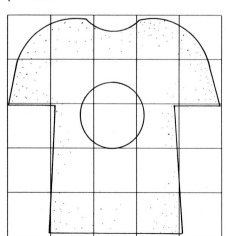

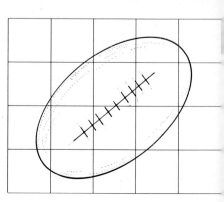

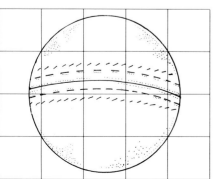

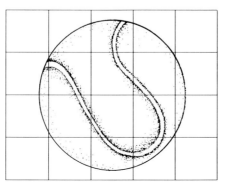

BALLERINA

This graceful ballerina cake, with daisy and ballet shoe biscuits is sure to enchant the birthday girl.

THE CAKE

2 x 200-mm (8-in) square cakes*, both 40-mm (1½-in) deep
butter icing*; 225 g (8 oz) flesh (mix a little yellow with pale pink); 125 g (4 oz) brown (use cocoa powder); 350 g (12 oz) white; 75 g (2½ oz) pink; 675 g (1½ lb) very pale blue (use white margarine)
piped flowers*, if desired

450 x 250-mm (18 x 10-in) cake board
sharp, smooth-bladed knife
9 paper piping bags
tubes: Ateco Nos. 1 and 2 writing, Nos. 16 and 18 star

1 Trace pattern and enlarge to measure 325 mm (13 in) from top of head to toe of shoe. Cut out, removing shaded triangles.

2 Place cakes on board and attach to each other and to board with butter icing.

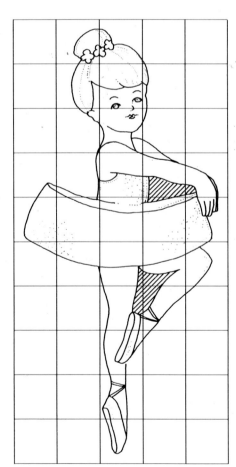

3 Pin pattern to cake with cocktail sticks. Cut vertically into cake around outline of pattern, taking care not to cut deeper than 15 mm (¾-in) below surface. Remove pattern.

4 Start at a corner and slice horizontally into cake at a depth of 15 mm (¾-in) until you reach cut outline of ballerina. Remove background cake from around ballerina. Repeat this process, cutting inwards from each corner, until all background is removed.

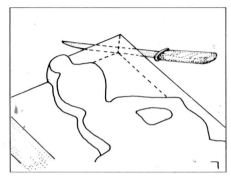

5 Soften 225 g (8 oz) flesh-coloured icing and spread over ballerina – surface and sides – but not on background. Leave to set.

6 Prick holes through pattern along lines of facial features. Place pattern on cake. Mark outline of cut-out triangles and mark facial features by gently pricking cake through holes in paper (use minimum pressure or icing will stick to pattern). Remove pattern.

7 Cut three semi-circles from sections of cake removed from background to form ballerina's tutu. Sandwich these together with butter icing and attach to ballerina. Give the layers a slight upward curve.

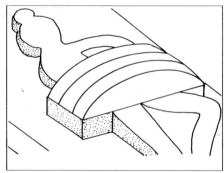

8 Pipe outline and details of figure on surface of cut-out ballerina, using brown icing and No. 2 tube. Pipe ballerina's hair with No. 16 tube, and facial features with No. 1 tube.

9 Use white icing and No. 16 tube to pipe stars* on bodice of dress, top (not edge) and underside of tutu. With a zigzag motion, pipe three rows of white 'frills' on edge of tutu, using No. 18 tube.

10 Soften 30 g (1 oz) pink icing with boiling water and place in paper piping bag with tip cut off. Cover ballet shoes with icing. Pipe shoe ribbons using pink icing with No. 2 tube. Pipe pink stars in ballerina's hair using No. 16 tube.

11 Flood* shaded triangles with softened pale blue icing in paper piping bag with tip cut off. Using No. 18 tube, pipe pale blue stars over background and sides of cake.

BALLET SHOE BISCUITS

10 pink sugar-coated almonds
10 white sugar-coated almonds
10 ginger nut biscuits
butter icing*: 125 g (4 oz) white; 200 g (7 oz) pink
royal icing*: 125 g (4 oz) each pink, white and blue (piped flowers*); 100 g (3½ oz) green (leaves*)

6 paper piping bags
tubes: Ateco No. 2 writing, No. 33 star (piped flowers)

1 Soften white butter icing and spread onto five ginger nut biscuits. Spread pink butter icing onto other five biscuits.

2 Attach two pink almonds to each white biscuit and two white almonds to each pink biscuit with icing.

3 Complete shoes by piping top rim of shoe, bow and ribbons with pink butter icing and No. 2 tube.

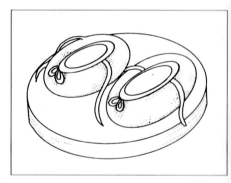

4 Decorate with leaves, piped with a V-cut piping bag*, and piped flowers*.

DAISY BISCUITS

10 birthday biscuits*, cut and baked in daisy shape (use cutter or template)
butter icing*: 100 g (3½ oz) pink; 100 g (3½ oz) white

2 paper piping bags
tube: Ateco No. 4 writing.

1 Pipe outline of biscuits with pink icing. Pipe central dot in white icing.

SPACESHIP

Fresh from a voyage to the stars, this fantasy cake and its accompanying 'men from Mars' will enchant the birthday child.

THE CAKE

225-mm (9-in) diameter round cake*
3 large cup cakes*
1 x 150-mm (6-in) diameter (at widest surface) dome-shaped cake*, baked in 75-mm (3-in) deep bowl
butter icing*: 150 g (5 oz) very pale blue; 100 g (3½ oz) dark blue; 450 g (1 lb) white

325-mm (13-in) round cake board
3 paper piping bags
tubes: Ateco No. 4 writing, No. 18 star
Smarties. red and brown
1 piece spaghetti, coloured with dark brown colouring

1 Place 225-mm (9-in) round cake on board. Cut each cup cake in half and attach all six, evenly spaced, to round cake with icing.

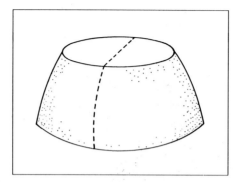

2 Attach dome cake to round cake with icing.

3 Soften 150 g (5 oz) very pale blue icing with a little boiling water and spread evenly over entire dome.

4 Using dark blue icing and No. 18 tube, pipe rows of stars* to form window frames on dome, starting at centre top.

5 Pipe squares and lines on each half cup cake with dark blue icing and No. 4 tube.

6 Fill in squares on half cup cakes with dark blue stars, piped with No. 18 tube.

7 Cover remainder of spaceship, and outline windows on dome with stars, using white icing and No. 18 tube.

8 Add red and black Smartie 'lights' and break piece of spaghetti in half to form radar/aerials.

'MEN FROM MARS' LOLLIPOPS

You can create a variety of interesting outer space characters using the methods below.

10 lollipops
marshmallow paste*: 30 g (1 oz) each green; white; blue; purple; yellow; 15 g (½ oz) black
black food colouring

paintbrush (5/0)
craft knife
modelling tool

Man from Mars 1 (green and purple)

1 Roll ball of marshmallow paste about size of large marble.

2 Press ball onto lollipop and shape with fingers, pulling out an ear on either side of face. Pull paste upwards to form top of head and downwards to form chin. Make a hole on each side of top of head.

3 Form two black marshmallow paste 'horns' and allow to dry. Dampen ends with water and insert in holes on head.

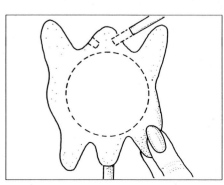

4 Paint on facial features with black food colouring.

Man from Mars 2 (yellow, white and blue)

1 Roll two sausages of marshmallow paste and make a ball on the end of each to form 'antennae'. Allow to dry.

2 Roll ball of marshmallow paste about size of large marble. Press onto lollipop and flatten into rectangular shape.

3 Turn lollipop face down and square off sides of head using craft knife.

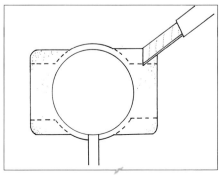

4 Roll two small balls of paste, flatten and hollow out to form ears. Dampen edges with water and attach to head.

5 Make two small holes in top of head using modelling tool.

6 Dampen base of dry 'antennae' with a little water and insert in holes. Paint on eye using black food colouring.

HAPPY HOLIDAYS

Brighten up a summer birthday party with this smiling, sunny cake. Ice-cream wafer cones and crunchy beach balls and sundaes add a festive touch.

THE CAKE

1 x 250-mm (10-in) diameter round cake*, 50-mm (2-in) deep
butter icing*: 200 g (7-oz) brown; 450 g (1 lb) yellow; 200 g (7 oz) orange
chocolate vermicelli

300-mm (12-in) round cake board
waxed paper
3 paper piping bags
tubes: Ateco No. 4 writing, No. 18 star

1 Cut a 250-mm (10-in) diameter circle out of paper. Fold circle in half. Fold paper in half two more times. Lay out flat – you should have eight divisions.

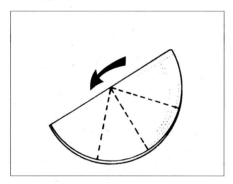

2 Copy pattern of sun face onto paper (inner circle has a diameter of 150 mm, 6 in) and cut out. Attach pattern to cake with cocktail sticks.

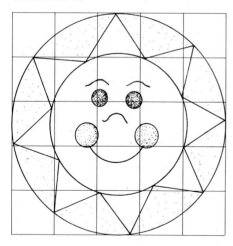

3 Cut rays of sun, holding knife vertically and taking care not to cut deeper than 15 mm (¾ in) below cake surface. Hold knife horizontally and undercut the triangles between rays. Remove triangles of cake, and pattern.

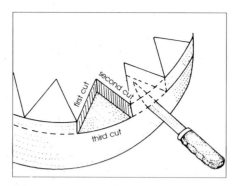

4 Pour chocolate vermicelli onto waxed paper. Soften 125 g (4 oz) brown icing with boiling water and spread thinly over sides of cake.

5 Gently roll cake over vermicelli to coat iced sides.

6 Soften 75 g (2½ oz) yellow icing and spread on vertical sides of rays of sun and over centre circle.

7 Using brown icing and No. 4 tube pipe around centre circle of cake. Mark eyes, eyebrows, nose, mouth and cheeks with a cocktail stick.

8 Pipe stars* on top surface of rays of sun and on cheeks, using orange icing and No. 18 tube.

9 Pipe eyes, eyebrows, nose and mouth using brown icing and No. 4 tube.

10 Use yellow icing and No. 18 tube to pipe stars on face and on triangular surfaces between rays of sun.

ICE-CREAM CONE BISCUITS

5 wafer biscuits
8 marshmallows
butter icing*: 100 g (3½ oz) white or pink

scissors
1 small paper piping bag

1 Cut wafer biscuits diagonally in half. Dipping blades of scissors in boiling water, cut each marshmallow into four discs.

2 Set aside 20 marshmallow discs and, on remaining discs, cut one side to form a point, as shown.

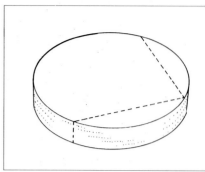

3 Attach two full marshmallow discs to each wafer 'cone' using butter icing. Attach pointed disc at the top.

4 Pipe 'drips of ice-cream' on 'cones' using icing in a paper piping bag with the tip cut off.

BEACH BALLS AND SUNNY SUNDAES

10 birthday biscuits* cut and baked in 65-mm (2¾-in) diameter circles for beach balls
10 birthday biscuits cut and baked in sundae shapes

beach balls:
royal icing*: 90 g (3 oz) each red; green; yellow

sunny sundaes:
royal icing*: 125 g (4 oz) pink, yellow, green or chocolate; 60 g (2 oz) white
butter icing*: 225 g (8 oz) white
3 drinking straws, each cut into 4 pieces

5-6 paper piping bags
tube: Ateco No. 2 writing

1 Outline and flood* biscuits.

2 When flooded sundaes have set, place butter icing in paper piping bag and cut 5 mm (¼ in) off tip. Pipe frothy top onto sundaes using a circular motion. Insert piece of drinking straw into butter icing.

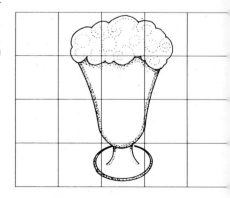

MISTER MOUSE

Add a touch of cartoon fun to the birthday feast with this bright mouse cake and a batch of tasty toadstool biscuits, cheese cookies and mouse lollies (see photograph on cover).

THE CAKE

1 x 300 x 225-mm (12 x 9-in) rectangular cake*
butter icing*: 675 g (1½ lb) beige; 225 g (8 oz) brown; 125 g (4 oz) pink; 125 g (4 oz) yellow; 75 g (2½ oz) red; 125 g (4 oz) white

350 x 275-mm (14 x 11-in) cake board
6 paper piping bags
tubes: Ateco No. 4 writing, No. 18 star
3 lengths spaghetti, coloured with dark brown colouring

2 Place cake on board and pin pattern to cake with cocktail sticks. Cut cake around pattern, then remove pattern. Attach bow tie.

3 Soften 225 g (8 oz) beige icing with 25 ml (5 tsp) boiling water. Spread thinly over top of cake. Allow to set.

4 Prick holes in paper pattern along lines of hat and features. Place pattern over set icing and transfer markings by gently pricking cake through holes in paper (use minimum pressure). Remove pattern.

5 Spread white icing over the area of the eyes. Pipe outline of eyes and centres with brown icing and No. 4 tube.

6 With beige icing and No. 18 tube pipe stars* on face and around ears. With pink icing and No. 18 tube pipe stars in centre of ears.

7 Pipe nose and mouth using brown icing and No. 4 tube.

8 With brown icing and No. 18 tube pipe stars on hat. Pipe stars on hat band and bow tie excluding polka dots) with yellow icing and No. 18 tube. Pipe red polka dots on bow tie with red icing and No. 18 tube.

9 Break three lengths of spaghetti in half and colour them by wiping them with a piece of cotton wool dipped in brown colouring. Insert them in cake as whiskers.

CHEESE WEDGE BISCUITS AND TOADSTOOL MOUSE HOUSES

10 birthday biscuits*, cut and baked as cheese wedges (make template*)
10 birthday biscuits*, cut and baked in toadstool shape (make template*)

cheese wedges:
royal icing*: 175 g (6 oz) yellow; 30 g (1 oz) brown

toadstool mouse houses:
royal icing*: 60 g (2 oz) yellow; 175 g (6 oz) red; 30 g (1 oz) brown
3 paper piping bags
tube: Ateco No 2. writing

1 Outline and flood* biscuits. Add details.

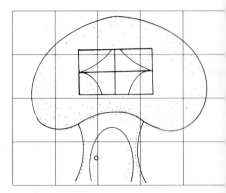

MOUSE FAMILY LOLLIPOPS

10 lollipops
marshmallow paste*: 75 g (2½ oz) flesh (pink and yellow mixed); 30 g (1 oz) each pink; white; black; brown; red; yellow

board to roll paste on
plastic roller
craft knife
black colouring
pink dusting powder (available from specialist cake decorating shops)
paintbrush (5/0)

1 Follow instructions for modelling lollies* making faces in flesh colour.

2 Make ears using shaped balls of flesh-coloured and pink paste.

3 Use small, flattened ovals of white paste for whites of eyes, and flattened balls of black paste for centres.

4 Roll tiny ball of black paste for nose.

5 Brush cheeks with pink powder and paint on mouth and whiskers with black food colouring.

6 Using illustration as a guide, complete lollies by moulding hats, bows and ties and attaching to lollies.

1 Trace pattern and enlarge to fit onto cake. Cut out pattern.

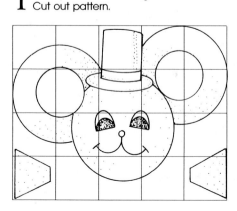

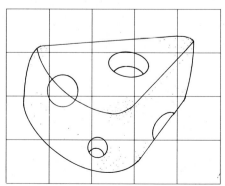

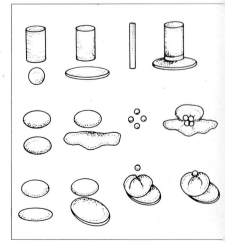